science QUEST

NATIONAL
GEOGRAPHIC   Washington D.C.

Atomic Universe

The Quest to Discover Radioactivity

Kate Boehm Jerome

Marie Curie working in her lab in 1905.

CONTENTS

The *Buffalo*, a nuclear-powered attack submarine, goes underwater while conducting tests at sea.

INTRODUCTION

A poor young woman…an accidental discovery…people poisoned by unknown danger. Sounds like the plot of a mystery. And, in a way it is. But this is the true story of how we came to know about radioactivity. Today people use radioactivity to treat cancer, study fossils, and even power submarines. However, radioactivity was discovered less than 150 years ago.

1800

The United States government moves from Philadelphia to its new capital, Washington, D.C.

1816

A French doctor named R.T. Laennec invents the stethoscope.

1817

The elements cadmium, lithium, and selenium are discovered.

> Scientists raced to find new information. It was an exciting time to do research.

Building knowledge about science can be a surprising process. It involves great new ideas, but hard work and good luck often play just as big a role. And in the 1800s, there were many people who were greatly interested in science and its emerging role in the world.

On cold winter nights in the 19th century, most families gathered around the stove or the fireplace to keep warm. People read books by lamplight and candlelight. There was much talk about an American fellow named Thomas Edison. People said that his new invention—the electric lightbulb—could brighten a room with the flick of a switch. Horses and buggies carried people along crowded city streets. A new machine, however, would soon chug noisily onto the scene. People called it the automobile. This "horseless carriage" would rule the roads of the future. It would change transportation forever.

A painting of the inside of a farmhouse in the 1800s.

Education was important, but many students, especially girls, did not graduate from high school. In fact, women were not allowed to attend college in many places around the world. New medical discoveries were being made all the time. Doctors were starting to understand how germs made people sick. They even said that some illnesses could be prevented if people washed their hands more often.

Scientists raced to find new information. It was an exciting time to do research. And it was a particularly exciting time for a chemist named Dmitry Mendeleyev.

An illustration of Dmitry Mendeleyev thinking at his desk in the chemical laboratory of the University of St. Petersburg.

AN ORDER TO THE ELEMENTS

Dmitry Mendeleyev taught chemistry at a university in St. Petersburg, Russia. He was so interested in his work, he often paid little attention to anything else— including himself. It was quite common to see Professor Mendeleyev with wild long hair, a scraggly beard, and messy clothing. He didn't care. He was thinking!

Dmitry Mendeleyev

BORN February 8, 1834
Tobolsk, Siberia, Russia

DIED February 2,1907
St. Petersburg, Russia

Dmitry Mendeleyev was the youngest of 17 children. After his father died, Dmitry and his family left Siberia in search of a better life.

The Mendeleyev family settled in St. Petersburg. While living there, Dmitry became very interested in chemistry. He wanted to understand the properties of all the elements known at the time. He organized them into a chart that is now known as the Periodic Table of Elements. In 1871, Mendeleyev left gaps in the chart for the discovery of new elements. He predicted that elements would be found to fill the gaps, and he was right. It was a wise decision. Three more elements were discovered within 20 years. Today, more than 100 elements have been discovered.

1834 Dmitry Mendeleyev is born.

1845 Wilhelm Roentgen is bor

An Expert on Elements

Dmitry Mendeleyev was born in Tobolsk, Siberia. He grew up in a large family with sixteen brothers and sisters. Dmitry was the youngest.

Mendeleyev's mother ran a glass factory to support the family. Dmitry used to spend time watching the glass being made. He was a curious boy and asked many questions. When Dmitry was in his early teens, hard times struck. Dmitry's father died, and the glass factory burned to the ground. But Dmitry's mother was still strong. She decided to take Dmitry to a big city. She knew he needed a college education to be successful.

At the University of St. Petersburg, Dmitry studied chemistry. He was particularly interested in the elements—substances made up of only one kind of atom. People had been studying elements, such as iron and gold, since ancient times. They knew that different elements, or combinations of elements, made up everything in the world—just as different letters, or combinations of letters, make up every word in the English language.

Henri Becquerel
is born.

The University of St.
Petersburg in Russia.

In the 1860s, 63 elements had been discovered—
and Dmitry Mendeleyev collected information on all
of them. He didn't know it at the time, but his work
set the stage for many exciting discoveries.

Predicting the Future

Mendeleyev spent many years gathering information
about the elements. He did research on his own. He also
studied the work of other scientists from all over the
world. His eagerness to share information was important.
Sometimes, scientists in Russia did not communicate
with scientists elsewhere in Europe. But Mendeleyev
needed as much information as he could get.

In the 1860s, 63
elements had been
discovered—and
Dmitry Mendeleyev
collected informa-
tion on all of them.

Dmitry Mendeleyev's periodic table is now carved into the side of a technical school in Russia.

Dmitry's hard work was beginning to pay off. He began to see patterns among the elements. He suspected that elements could be grouped together, and he figured out a way to group them. Dmitry organized each known element in a chart by taking the atomic weight of an atom from each element and putting the elements in order of lightest to heaviest. For example, hydrogen has an atomic weight of about one atomic mass unit, which makes it the lightest element, and the first element on the table. Finally, in 1869, Dmitry Mendeleyev unveiled an organized table of elements. He listed the 63 known elements of the time. He also left blank spaces for three more elements, which he predicted would one day be discovered.

1861

U.S. Civil War begins.

1859

Pierre Curie is born.

1867

Marie Curie is born.

Most people thought he was crazy, but it turned out that Mendeleyev was right. By 1886, three new elements had been found. They fit right into the gaps that Mendeleyev had left in his table.

Mendeleyev's table brought order to the way scientists thought about the elements, and proved that many things were yet to be discovered. Today, this table is known as the Periodic Table of Elements.

A child in Poland grew up to be inspired by Mendeleyev's work. As an adult, this scientist added two new elements to Mendeleyev's table. This person also became the first ever to be awarded two Nobel Prizes. These achievements alone were amazing. And the fact that this scientist was a woman was absolutely astonishing.

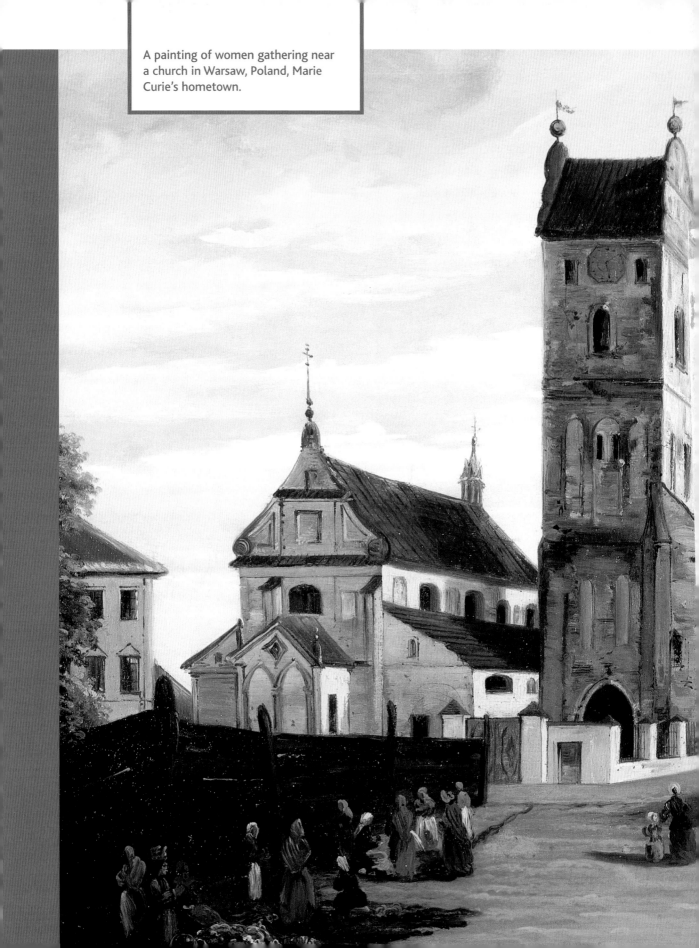

A painting of women gathering near a church in Warsaw, Poland, Marie Curie's hometown.

BREAKING NEW GROUND

In the 1800s, many teachers believed women were not very smart. They thought that since a woman's brain is smaller than a man's, a woman could not understand complex things. For example, some men thought that a woman could take scientific notes, but they did not think she could understand her notes. Luckily, many women of the day—including Marie Curie—knew better.

Marie Curie

BORN November 7, 1867
Warsaw, Poland

DIED July 4, 1934
Sallanches, France

Marie Curie was a bright young girl, always eager to learn. Her father was her first teacher and encouraged Marie and her siblings to discover new things. Marie graduated from high school when she was 15 and went on to study at the Sorbonne University in Paris. There she became the first woman to earn a degree in physics.

In 1895, Marie married Pierre Curie and together they researched radioactive elements. They won a Nobel Prize for physics in 1903, along with Henry Becquerel. Marie won a second Nobel Prize in 1911 for the discovery of radium. She became the first person to win two

1879
Thomas Edison invents the lightbulb.

1882
A German doctor named Robert Koch discovers tuberculosis.

An Early Love of Learning

Marie Curie was born Manya Sklodowska on November 7, 1867, in Warsaw, Poland. Everyone called her Manya. At this time in history, Russia ruled Poland, and the official language of the country was Russian. Manya and her friends had to do their schoolwork in Russian—not in their native language of Polish. Sometimes the Polish students got low grades from their Russian teachers. Manya and her brother and three sisters were bright. Their father, a teacher, encouraged them to read and ask questions. He brought books home, and he talked about science and history. He wanted his children to be curious about the world.

Manya loved to learn. She did well with her studies. She graduated from high school at age 15 with a medal for being the best in her class. Manya had big plans to continue her education. She also had a big problem. Universities in Poland did not accept women.

The Sorbonne University in Paris.

Struggling for an Education

There was one university in Europe that did accept women. It was called the Sorbonne, and it was located in Paris, France. Manya and her sister were determined to attend the Sorbonne. Going to the university was expensive, so the girls decided to save money and send Bronya first. Then, after Bronya graduated, she would work to help pay for Manya's education.

While Manya was working in Warsaw, she attended a secret night school called the "Floating University." Here educated Polish people shared their knowledge with each other. They hoped that Poland would one day be free of Russian rule. Manya knew it was dangerous to attend the school, but her desire to learn was stronger than her fear.

science BOOSTER

Fun Fact
Manya heard stories about the chemist Dmitry Mendeleyev while studying at the museum in Warsaw. Manya's cousin, who was a teacher there, had worked for the famous Russian scientist.

Marie (second from the left) with her brother Jozio (center) and sisters Hela (left) and Bronya (right).

Manya also studied at a museum in Warsaw where she did her first chemistry experiments. The work was very exciting, and Manya's interest in science began to grow.

After her sister became a doctor, it was Manya's turn to attend the Sorbonne. In France, Manya decided to use the French version of her name—Marie.

Overcoming Challenges

Although she loved Paris, Marie faced many challenges. The other students were better educated than she was. Marie had to study very hard to catch up. And she was also doing all of her work in yet another language—French!

1886

The Statue of Liberty is unveiled in New York Harbor.

science BIOGRAPHY

Pierre Curie

BORN May 15, 1859
Paris, France

DIED April 19, 1906
Paris, France

Pierre Curie was educated at home by his father. He came from a poor background and didn't have the money to go to college right away. Instead, he became a lab instructor.

Pierre worked in the lab with his older brother Jacques. They did a lot of reaseach on how electricity affects compressed crystals. After several years, Pierre went to study at the Sorbonne, where he earned his doctorate degree in science in 1895. He then became a physics professor.

In 1894, Pierre met Marie; they married in 1895. Their world-famous scientific partnership led to the discovery of two elements—radium and polonium.

Marie had very little money. For a time she lived with her sister. After moving out of her sister's house, she lived in a tiny attic that was cold in the winter and hot in the summer. She barely had enough to eat. But Marie didn't mind. She studied all the time.

In 1893 Marie became the first woman to receive a degree in physics from the Sorbonne University. She also received the highest grade in her class and proved to the world that a woman could understand science just as well as a man.

Marie planned to return to Poland, but something happened to change her mind. Friends introduced Marie to a French scientist named Pierre Curie. They talked for hours about science. Soon a romance began, and on July 26, 1895, Marie married Pierre. Their wedding not only made them husband and wife, but it also created a great scientific partnership.

When they were not doing research,
Pierre and Marie enjoyed riding bicycles.

The ferris wheel is introduced at the World's Fair in Chicago.

Marie with her two daughters, Irène and Ève.

The Curies led a busy life. Both taught at the university, worked in the laboratory, and continued studying. In 1897 they became parents of their first child, Irène; but Marie did not give up her work. In fact, she decided to continue teaching and get an advanced degree in physics.

Marie's decision to continue her education in science was very unusual at the time. Marie didn't care what other people thought. She had a new challenge to focus on. To earn her advanced degree, she needed to do some original research. And her choice of study would change her life, and many others, forever.

> To earn her advanced degree, Marie needed to do some original research.

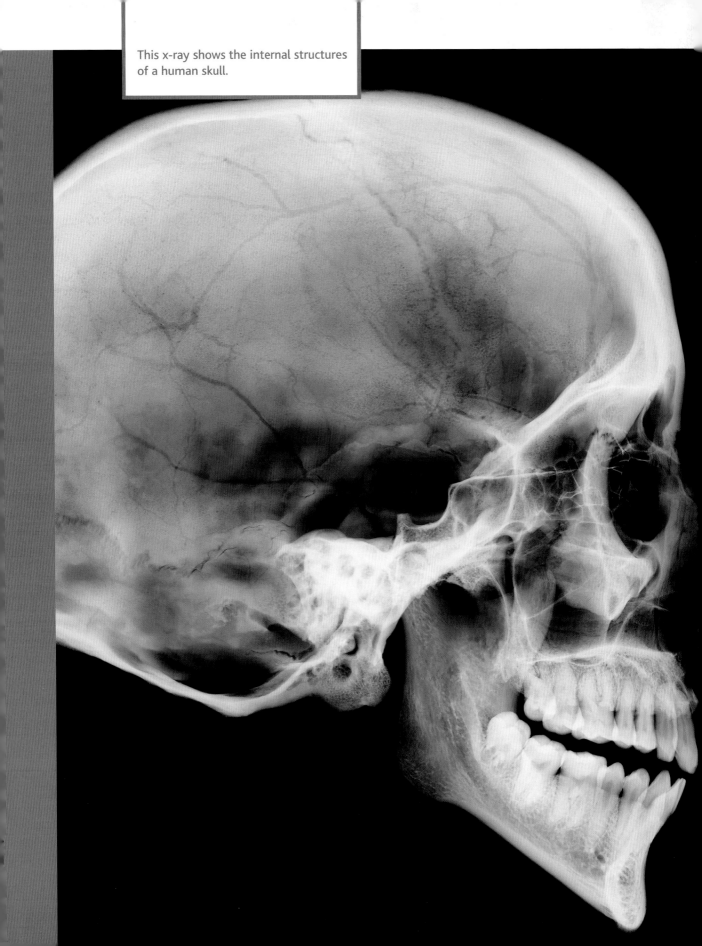

This x-ray shows the internal structures of a human skull.

A DISCOVERY CHANGES THE SCIENCE WORLD

In 1895, the same year that Marie and Pierre Curie were married, a German scientist announced an astonishing discovery. Wilhelm Roentgen found that a mysterious ray could pass through wood, metal, even human flesh. Roentgen named this strange ray the x-ray because scientists often used "x" to represent something unknown.

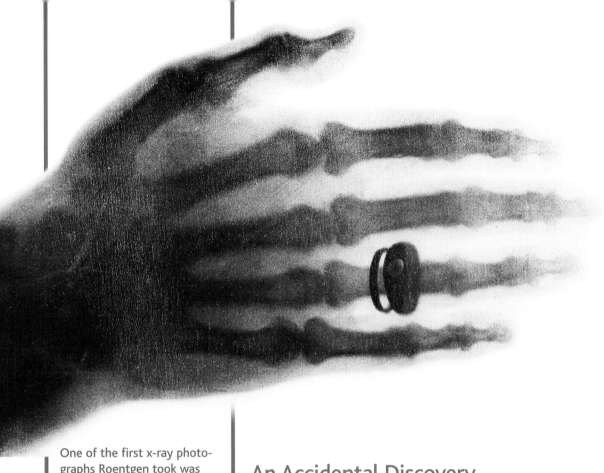

One of the first x-ray photographs Roentgen took was of his wife's hand. You can clearly see her ring.

An Accidental Discovery

Roentgen had discovered x-rays by accident. One night he was working in his lab with something called a "Crooke's tube." When electricity was passed through the tube, it gave off a faint glow caused by special rays called cathode rays. At one point Roentgen covered the Crooke's tube with black cardboard. Suddenly, he noticed that a screen more than six feet (two meters) away from the tube was glowing. Roentgen knew cathode rays couldn't travel that far. A different kind of ray must be causing the glow. Roentgen stuck his hand in the path of the invisible beam. He was shocked. He saw his own bones reflected on the screen!

At first Roentgen kept his discovery a secret. He did not want to tell anyone that he could take pictures of the bones inside their bodies. He knew it would be very hard for people to believe.

> For the first time, doctors could look inside bodies without cutting them open.

science BIOGRAPHY

Wilhelm Roentgen

BORN March 27, 1845
Lennep, Prussia (now Germany)

DIED February 10, 1923
Munich, Germany

Wilhelm Roentgen was born in 1845 to a cloth maker, and at age three, his family moved to the Netherlands. Although Wilhelm was a good student, he was expelled from school after being accused of drawing a caricature of one of his teachers, but he insisted that the claim was false.

He entered college in 1865, and in 1876 Whilhelm became a physics professor. He spent his time teaching and conducting research, and in 1895, while studying electrical currents, Whilhelm discovered the x-ray. His discovery captivated the world.

In 1901, Wilhelm received the first Nobel Prize in physics for his discovery.

Besides, Roentgen was a careful scientist. He wanted to do more experiments. So he spent weeks testing x-rays and collecting more data. Finally, Roentgen wrote a scientific paper. He announced his work and described the new x-rays in detail. His findings brought almost immediate attention, and people began clamoring for more information on what Roentgen had learned.

X-rays Wow the World

Marie and Pierre Curie were thrilled to learn about the mysterious x-rays. Public interest was very high. Soon people began to think of ways to use this new scientific discovery. X-rays quickly changed the field of medicine. For the first time, doctors could look inside bodies without cutting them open. Broken bones were now easy to see. Metal objects, such as bullets, could be located quickly.

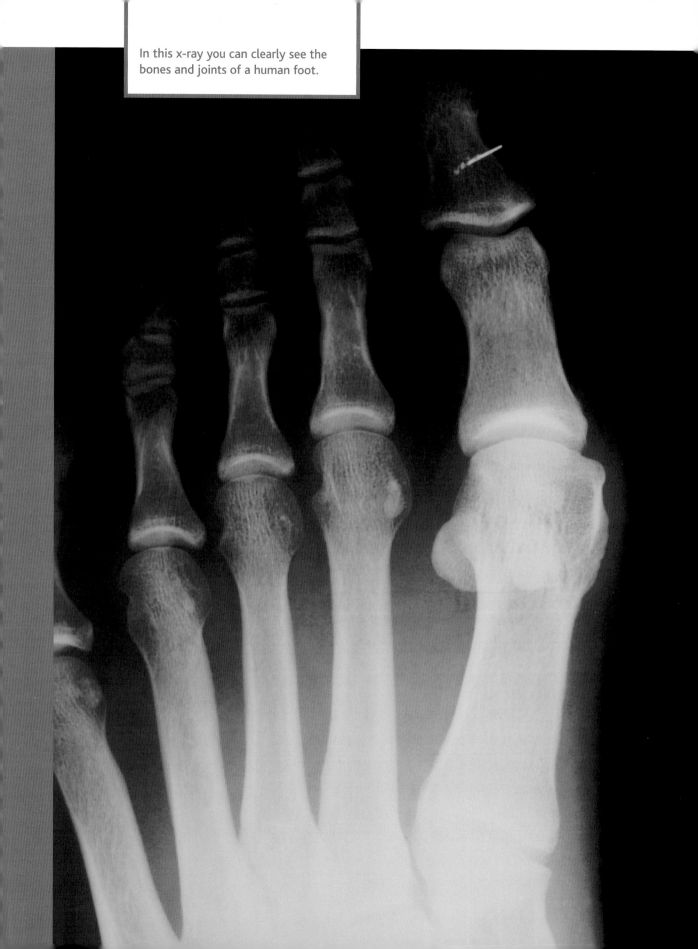

In this x-ray you can clearly see the bones and joints of a human foot.

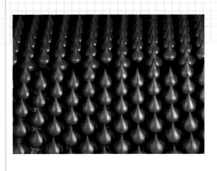

1894

Milton Hershey starts the Hershey Chocolate Company.

1893

New Zealand becomes the first country to allow women the right to vote in national elections.

Some people took the use of x-rays even further. They wanted pictures of their bones to be displayed as artwork. They didn't yet know of the possible dangers of the newly discovered rays. In fact, when the side effect of hair loss was reported, some people took it as a good thing. Perhaps, they thought, x-rays might be used instead of daily shaving!

The Mystery of "Uranic Rays"

A Frenchman named Henri Becquerel began to study x-rays. Becquerel knew that x-rays had to come from some source, and he wanted to uncover just what that source was. Becquerel took photographic plates and wrapped them in black paper. He then placed uranium crystals on top of the plates and put them in sunlight. When he developed the plates, Becquerel could see that the crystals were giving off rays that darkened the plates.

> Becquerel knew that x-rays had to come from some source, and he wanted to uncover just what that source was.

STRAND-JDYLL Á LA F

A cartoon poking fun at x-rays. It was published in 1900, five years after x-rays were discovered.

At first, Becquerel thought that the sunlight made the uranium crystals give off rays. But one day he made a discovery. He developed a plate that had crystals on it but had not been in the sun. The plate was still darkened. This meant that the uranium crystals did not need the sun. They were giving off rays that could go through matter all on their own. Becquerel called these rays "uranic rays," because he thought they came from the uranium in the crystals.

1895 | X-rays discovered.

1900 | Boxer Rebellion occurs in China.

science BIOGRAPHY

Henri Becquerel

BORN December 15, 1852
Paris, France

DIED August 25, 1908
Le Croisic, France

Henry Becquerel was born into a family of distinguished scientists. This helped fuel his early interest in science. He studied engineering and worked for many years as an engineer.

Henri also assisted his father at the Museum of Natural History. After his father's death, Henri focused his research on infrared radiation. In 1896, while working with phosphorescence in how uranium salts glow, he noticed that uranium emits rays. No one paid much attention to his findings until Marie and Pierre Curie investigated and realized that he had in fact discovered radioactivity. In 1903, Henri and the Curies shared the Nobel Prize for the discovery.

He began to publish papers and make speeches about the rays. But no one paid much attention to his discovery. Everyone was still too interested in x-rays—everyone, that is, except Marie Curie. Marie was still searching for a good topic to study for her advanced degree. Since few people were paying attention to Becquerel's "uranic rays," she decided that they would be a perfect subject for her study.

It was a great decision. Marie Curie was about to figure out that Becquerel had accidentally discovered radioactivity.

This laboratory, built in 1914, was where Marie conducted her research while working at the Radium Institute of Paris.

CURIE TAKES ON THE CHARGE

Marie was excited about studying "uranic rays." All she needed was a laboratory. Pierre's boss came to the rescue. He provided Marie with a small room to work in. When she needed more space, Marie moved to a nearby shed. It was drafty and had a leaky roof, but Marie didn't care. She finally had her own lab.

Pierre and Marie working together, researching radioactive materials in their lab

Unraveling the Mystery

Marie tried to learn more about Becquerel's "uranic rays." It wasn't easy. The rays couldn't be seen. In fact, they could only be detected on photographic plates or when they made the air conduct electricity.

Marie took advantage of her science partnership with her husband. Pierre and his brother had invented a machine that measured weak electric currents. Marie borrowed the machine and tested different rock samples to see if they produced the same rays as Becquerel's uranium-containing crystals. She found that another element, called thorium, gave off rays that were like Becquerel's. She worked more with uranium samples. Marie soon realized that the "uranic rays" were stronger when there was more uranium in a sample. She also learned that the rays did not come from stored-up heat or light. Temperature did not affect them, either.

1903

Marie and Pierre Curie and Henri Becquerel win the Nobel Prize for their work on radioactivity.

1905

Ground is broken for the Panama Canal.

Then Marie had an idea. What if the rays were coming from the uranium and thorium atoms themselves? This would mean that Marie had discovered a new property of matter. A discovery this important had to have a name. Marie called the new property "radioactivity." This word comes from the Latin word radius, meaning "ray."

The Hard Work Continues

Marie studied dozens of different substances. She was especially interested in a substance called pitchblende. Marie found that pitchblende was very radioactive. Surprisingly, pitchblende was still radioactive even after Marie took most of the uranium out of it. This was a puzzle. Marie thought she had made a mistake. So she tested the pitchblende again and again. She kept getting the same results. Something else in the pitch-blende was giving off radiation. But no other known element in pitchblende was radioactive, and Marie began to wonder if there was another radioactive element that had yet to be uncovered.

The first Nobel Prizes were awarded in 1901 at this ceremony in Stockholm, Sweden. Pierre and Marie received their awards two years later.

Pierre Curie was impressed with his wife's work. After just three months of research, Marie was about to discover a new element. Pierre decided to help Marie. Together they worked even harder.

Marie and Pierre knew the new element must exist in only very tiny amounts. To get at it, they had to break down the pitchblende. They ground up the pitchblende and put it into a huge iron pot. They added chemicals to the pot to break down the pitchblende some more. They heated the pot over a fire, and Marie had to stir the mixture and add wood to the fire to keep it hot. Fumes stung her eyes and throat. The work was exhausting.

Discovering a New Element

After working with the pitchblende for three months, the
Curies finally had a black powder that was very radioactive, and they found that it did contain the new element.
Marie decided to name the element "polonium" in honor
of Poland—the country of her birth.

The discovery of polonium was exciting, but more exciting
news was about to come. After a few more months
of research, Marie and Pierre were sure that pitchblende
contained not one, but two radioactive elements. On
December 26, 1898, the Curies published a report on a
second new element. They named the element "radium."

After several more years of hard work with the new elements, Marie and Pierre finally were able to get pure
samples of polonium and radium.

In November 1903, Marie, Pierre, and Henry Becquerel
learned that they had won a Nobel Prize in physics for
their work on radioactivity.

Pitchblende is a mineral that
contains polonium and radium.

science BOOSTER

Did You Know?
Some elements have a
nucleus that is unstable.
The nucleus can break
down, or decay, to form a
different element with a
lighter nucleus. This decay
is called radioactivity.

Marie, Pierre, and their daughter, Irène

REWARDS, AND MORE DISCOVERIES

Marie and Pierre Curie were quiet people. They did not like all the publicity that came with winning the Nobel Prize. They were invited to travel and make speeches. People wanted to see them, but the Curies just wanted to be left alone. They wanted to continue their research.

1906

Pierre Curie dies.

1907

Dmitry Mendeleyev dies.

1908

Henri Becquerel dies.

> Pierre and Marie thought science should be shared with everyone.

Sharing the Discovery

The Curies were the only people in the world who knew how to get radium out of pitchblende. If Marie and Pierre decided to patent this process (to make it their own by law), they could make a lot of money. However, Pierre and Marie thought science should be shared with everyone. They would not keep the process to themselves. They freely explained it to anyone who asked. They would get by on the money they had.

Although the Curies' research was going well, they were both beginning to have health problems. Pierre often had terrible leg pains. Sometimes he could not get out of bed. Marie was always tired. Both Pierre and Marie knew that radium could cause burns. Their fingers were always sore and cracked from touching it. Was it possible the radioactive materials they handled every day were hurting them more than they knew?

Marie Curie converses with her colleague Albert Einstein. They met at international science conferences.

1909

The *New York Tir* publishes its firs movie review.

A painting of Paris at the turn of the 19th century.

Unfortunately, the answer was yes. They didn't know it, but both Pierre and Marie were suffering from radiation sickness. Their aches and pains and tiredness would be with them for the rest of their lives. In 1904, the Curies had another daughter. Marie was glad that her two girls, Eve and Irene, were healthy. Marie had a teaching job that she liked. Things seemed to be going well for the Curie family.

Tragedy Strikes

Then tragedy struck. On April 19, 1906, Pierre left for work as usual. It was rainy and cold. Pierre often did not pay much attention to his surroundings. He was too busy thinking about his research. That day, his absent-mindedness cost him his life. He stepped in front of a horse-drawn wagon. The driver could not stop. Pierre Curie was killed.

1912

The *Titanic* sinks.

1910

World population surpasses 1.5 billion.

Marie missed Pierre terribly. But she continued to work and raise her daughters as she knew Pierre would want her to. Then the Sorbonne University asked Marie to take over Pierre's teaching job. Marie would become the first woman professor at the Sorbonne. Marie agreed to do it, but it was hard to find joy in her life without Pierre.

Helping the World

In 1911, Marie Curie was awarded a Nobel Prize in chemistry for discovering radium and polonium. No one had ever won two Nobel Prizes. Marie was pleased, but she was more interested in another project. Before Pierre died, he had thought about using radium to cure cancer. Marie wanted to explore how radioactivity might help people. The French government agreed to build a research center so people could study the possibilities. Marie helped plan it. In 1914, the French Radium Institute was finished, and Marie finally had a first-rate laboratory.

> Marie would become the first woman professor at the Sorbonne.

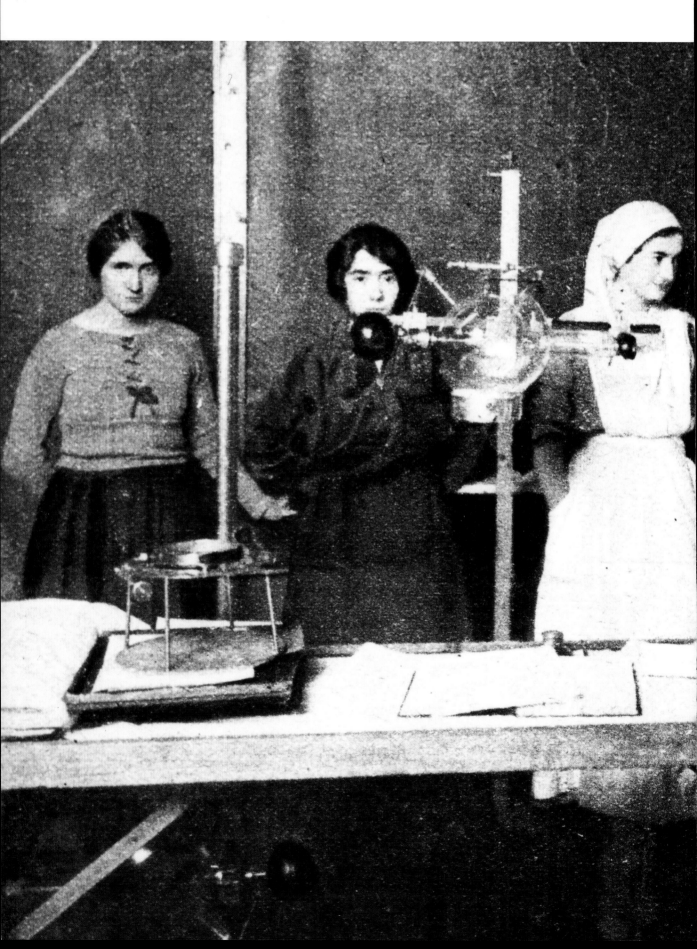

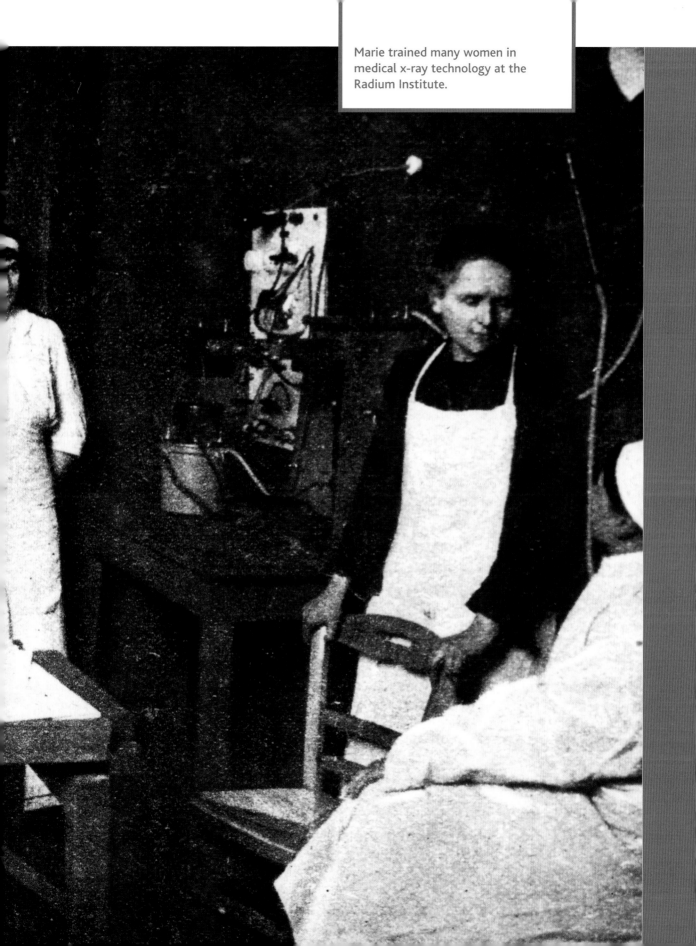

Marie trained many women in medical x-ray technology at the Radium Institute.

1914

World War I begins.

1927

Charles Lindbergh becomes the first pilot to fly solo across the Atlantic Ocean.

1923

Wilhelm Roentgen dies.

> At age 53, Marie traveled all over to talk to people about one of her favorite subjects— radioactivity.

As usual, however, things did not go exactly as planned for Marie. Before she could settle into her new work at the Radium Institute, World War I broke out. When the Germans invaded France, Marie decided to help in the war. She thought it was a good idea to put x-ray units in vans. Then they could be driven around to army hospitals. She knew that x-rays would be needed to help wounded soldiers. Once again, Marie's ideas had a big impact on many people.

Her Work Continues

After the war ended, Marie wanted to get back to her research. She made a trip to the United States to raise awareness and support for her work. She still didn't enjoy crowds, but she knew she should explain her science to other people. At age 53, Marie traveled all over to talk to people about one of her favorite subjects—radioactivity.

Marie Curie dies.

Marie met President Warren G. Harding on her trip to the United States.

During this time, other scientists added to the work that Marie had begun. Although Marie hadn't found the source of radioactivity, some were beginning to figure it out. One researcher in England, Ernest Rutherford, figured out that radioactive materials gave off different kinds of rays. This—and other research—led him to discover that an atom has a nucleus.

The Final Days

Marie kept up with all the latest research. In fact, her best times were still spent in her laboratory. But radiation sickness kept slowing her down. She had a constant buzzing in her ears, and she was always tired and weak.

On July 4, 1934, Marie Curie died of leukemia. The disease that killed her was most likely caused by the work that so enriched her life.

Explosions of atomic bombs produce giant mushroom clouds and cause great damage.

CONTRIBUTIONS

Around 440 B.C., a Greek philosopher named Democritus suggested the idea and name of the atom. For over 1400 years, people thought of the atom in the same way. Most scientists thought that the atom was the basic building block of all matter. It could not be divided, and nothing was smaller. The discovery of radioactivity changed all that. Why?

This nuclear power plant is located on the banks of the River Seine in France.

An Awesome Power

Radioactivity showed that things come out of atoms. This meant that atoms were not the smallest units of matter. Atoms had to be made up of even smaller particles. This was an astounding thought at the time. Once scientists began to think about the atom in a new way, it wasn't long before they figured out its structure. This led to another idea that changed our whole world. Scientists realized that awesome power could be released by splitting atoms. The age of atomic, or nuclear, power was born.

1945

During World War II the United States drops atomic bombs on Hiroshima and Nagasaki in Japan.

1971

Nuclear medicine is recognized as a medical specialty by the American Medical Association.

How We Came to Know

In some ways, the process of discovering radioactivity was just as important as the discovery itself. Good scientists were not afraid to keep asking questions and finding answers. For example, Dmitry Mendeleyev predicted that more elements would be found, even though some people thought they knew all the elements. Marie Curie could have given up the idea of getting an education because she was a woman. However, she knew she could make contributions to science, and she spent her entire life proving the point. Wilhelm Roentgen and Henri Becquerel were careful scientists who were smart enough to test unusual observations. These observations then led to unexpected discoveries.

The amount we know about science continually increases, and changes every day. There are still many more exciting discoveries to be made.

science BOOSTER

Fun Fact
Where could you find radioactivity today? For one thing, as Pierre and Marie Curie hoped, doctors can use radioactivity to treat cancer. It is also used to sterilize medical instruments and food, and produce energy for heat and electrical power.

Fuel rods, like the ones shown here, provide nuclear energy in a reactor.

GLOSSARY

Atom
the smallest particle of an element that has properties of the element

Chemist
a scientist who studies the properties, structure, and interaction of matter

Crystals
material composed of atoms that are arranged in repeating patterns

Electric current
the flow of electricity from one point to another

Element
a substance made of only one type of atom

Leukemia
a blood disease in which too many white blood cells are produced

Matter
the substance a physical object is composed of

Nucleus
the central part of an atom

Photographic plate
a glass plate used before the invention of camera film

Physics
the study of matter and energy

Pitchblende
a black mineral that contains uranium and other elements

Property
a quality that can define or describe something

Radioactivity
the breaking down, or decay, of the unstable nucleus of certain elements, which results in new elements with a lighter nucleus

Side effect
a usually unwanted symptom or medical problem

A colored image of radium particles. Radium is a very powerful radioactive substance.

Biographical Resources

Would you like to read about Marie Curie's discovery of uranium, in her own words? Visit http://womenshistory. about.com/od/quotes/a/ marie_curie.htm

Visit the Curie Museum online at http://www.curie.fr/foundation/musee/musee.cfm/lang/ _gb.htm to learn more about the work of Pierre and Marie Curie. There you'll also find photographs and lab notes dating back to 1902, showing the Curies' work on radium.

To read more about the experiments Wilhelm Roentgen conducted in his discovery of x-rays, go to http://nobelprize. org/physics/laureates/1901/ rontgen-bio.html.

Read about Dmitry Mendeleyev's work in his own words. Go to http://www.chem.msu.su/eng/ misc/mendeleev/welcome.html and read some of his original papers.

Learn about Henri Becquerel's early work, and dicover the other fascinating contributions he made to science. Visit http://www.britannica.com/nobel/micro/59_13.html.

Other Cool Science Stuff About Radioactivity

For an interactive look at the complete Periodic Table of Elements, visit www.chemicool.com.

To see some of the many uses for x-rays, as well as a look at some positive uses of uranium and radioactivity, go to http://www.niehs.nih.gov/kids/uranium.htm.

Interested in learning more about x-rays? Visit http://www.uhrad.com/kids.htm. You'll also be able to see cool x-rays of everything from plants to animals, and even x-rays of some nonliving things!

To learn more about Marie Curie's fight to educate the world about radioactivity, click on http://www.aip.org/history/curie/.

What More Can I Do?

Would you like to understand more about the structure of atoms? Go to www.pbs.org/wgbh/aso/tryit/atom/ to use the Atom Builder and construct your own atoms!

For some interactive games sure to increase your knowledge of the Periodic Table of Elements, visit http://education.jlab.org/indexpages/elementgames.html

Check out www.chem4kids.com for a great overview on all things related to atoms, the periodic table, and chemical reactions.

Also, try heading out to your local science museum or library for more information and fun facts.

RESOURCES

INDEX

Book design by KINETIK. The body
text of the book is set in Bliss Regular.
The display text is set in Filosofia.

Library of Congress
Cataloging-in-Publication Data

Jerome, Kate Boehm.
Atomic universe : the quest to discover
radioactivity / by Kate Boehm Jerome.
p. cm.— (Science quest)
Includes bibliographical
references and index.
Trade ISBN–10: 0-7922-5543-7
Trade ISBN–13: 978-0-7922-5543-7
Library ISBN–10: 0-7922-5544-5
Library ISBN–13: 978-0-7922-5544-4
1. Nuclear physics. 2. Nuclear energy.
I. Title. II. Series: Science quest
(National Geographic Society (U.S.))
QC776.J47 2006
539.7—dc22

2006001316

Cover: Cover: Science Museum/SSPL/The
Image Works; 4-5: Science Photo Library
/Photo Researchers; 6: © Bettmann
/Corbis; 8-9: © Corbis; 10: Library of
Congress; 11: Edward Owen/Art
Resource, NY; 12-13: © Bettmann
/Corbis; 14: © Bettmann/Corbis; 15: ©
Steve Raymer/Corbis; 16: © Steve
Raymer/Corbis; 17: © Bettmann/Corbis;
18-19: © Archivo Iconografico, S.A.
/Corbis; 20: W. F. Meggers Collection
/AIP/Photo Researchers; 21: © Paul
Almasy/Corbis; 22: ACJC-Curie and Joliot
Curie Fund; 23 (top): © Eyewire; 23 (bot-
tom): ACJC-Curie and Joliot Curie Fund;
24: © Bettmann/Corbis; 25: © Bettmann
/Corbis; 26-27: Science Photo Library
/Photo Researchers; 28: © Bettmann
/Corbis; 29: © Bettmann/Corbis; 30: ©
Photomorgana/Corbis; 31: © Richard T.
Nowitz/Corbis; 32: J-L Charmet/Photo
Researchers; 33: © Bettmann/Corbis;
34-35: © Bettmann/Corbis; 36: Physics
Today Collection/American Institute of
Physics/Science Photo Library/Photo
Researchers; 37: © Ted Spiegel/Corbis;
38: Astrid & Hanns-Frieder Michler/Photo
Researchers; 39: The Nobel Foundation;
40-41: © Corbis; 42: ACJC-Curie and Joliot
Curie Fund; 43: American Institute of
Physics/Science Photo Library/Photo
Researchers; 44: © Archivo Iconografico,
S.A./Corbis; 45: © Bettmann/Corbis; 46-47:
ACJC-Curie and Joliot Curie Fund; 48: ©
Hulton-Deutsch Collection/Corbis; 49: ©
Bettmann/Corbis; 50-51: U.S. Navy/Science
Photo Library/Photo Researchers; 52: Julia
Waterlow; Eye Ubiquitous/Corbis; 53: ©
Bettmann/Corbis; 54-55: © Yann Arthus-
Bertrand/Corbis; 56: © C. Powell, P. Fowler
& D. Perkins/Science Photo Library/Photo
Researchers.

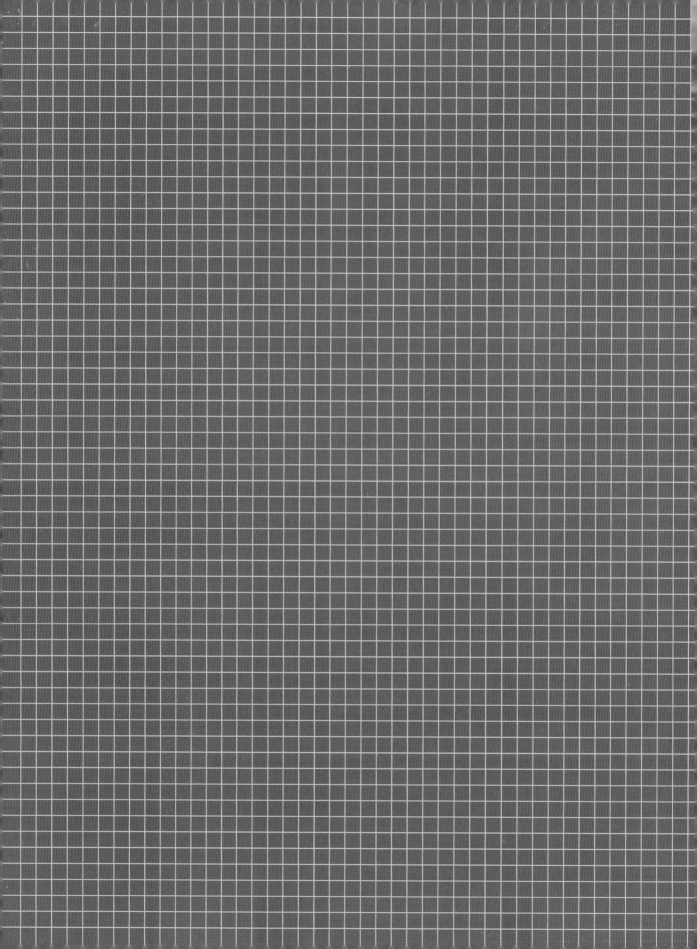